MEDITATIONS

for Women Physicians
(and Others)
Who Do Too Much

MEDITATIONS

for Women Physicians
(and Others)
Who Do Too Much

Robyn Alley-Hay, MD

©2022 by Robyn Alley-Hay, MD

All rights reserved. No part of this publication may be reproduced or transmitted in any form or by any means, electronic or mechanical, including photocopying, recording, or any other information storage and retrieval system, without the written permission of the author or publisher.

Internet addresses given in this book were accurate at the time it went to press.

This book is intended as a reference volume only, not as a medical manual. The information given here is designed to inspire and inform. It is not intended as a substitute for any treatment that may have been prescribed by your doctor. If you suspect that you have a medical problem, we urge you to seek competent medical help.

Printed in the United States of America
Published in Hellertown, PA
Cover and interior design and illustrations by

Library of Congress Control Number: 2022906866
ISBN: 978-1-952481-91-8
2 4 6 8 10 9 7 5 3 1

For more information or to place bulk orders, contact the publisher at Jennifer@BrightCommunications.net.

BrightCommunications.net

To my greatest teachers, Sean, Sam, Drew, and Allie

Please call your mother.

Author's Note

This book is written for all the workaholics, rushaholics, careaholics, busyaholics, perfectionists, overachievers, and those that feel somehow stuck in their lives/careers. You are my people. I happen to know that you are badass, powerful, intelligent, fun, and generally lovely. I wrote this book in case you forget or have forgotten.

May you have peace
May you have love
May you have joy
May you have equanimity

Introduction

This is how my career went...start medical school, get married, get pregnant, stop for a year. Start again second year, stop because of hyperemesis, miscarry that second trimester baby. Start medical school again, have my second baby over the summer break. Start Ob/Gyn residency, stop to have my third baby, have postpartum depression, take a short leave, start residency again. Finally finish residency and start private practice. Have baby number four and get fired from that first job (it was really a mutual separation); start again with husband as sole partner in a private practice, stop to stay home with all the kids, get divorced, be admitted to a mental hospital for depression, start practice again, start again, and start again. This was not how I dreamed my career and my life would turn out! But it is my life: the path I've taken, and I believe, the lessons my soul needed.

As women physicians, we end up crazy busy! This is the reality of so many in the current dysfunctional health care system. Being overly busy comes to be a normal part of being a female physician. We work hard, sacrifice, take care of everyone but ourselves and then wonder what is wrong when we feel depleted. I know I've wasted so much time in the pursuit of having the perfect career and life. When it didn't work, I naturally thought the problem was with me.

I should work harder, be better, happier, stronger. Little did I know that I was not alone, but part of an epidemic of too busy women physicians who struggle under the weight the demands the current healthcare system requires. For me, too busy at work translated to too busy at home and that led to feelings of guilt for not doing either very well. The spiral was definitely downward until I looked up and found my life unmanageable. It was not until I admitted that I could not do it all that I got the help I needed and started to heal. We cannot change the healthcare system before we heal ourselves.

The healing process allowed me to create a life that I love that is joyful, interesting, challenging, meaningful, and filled with adventure, accomplishment, happiness, and much love (including self-love)! I still deal with depression once in a while, and I still lose socks in the laundry even though my kids are grown, but there are so many good days that I appreciate to the fullest. I want this for you, too. This book is composed of wisdoms and my personal thoughts that may get you started on that path. You don't go through years of therapy and coaching and not come away with some wisdom! I share what wisdom I have with you, my dear reader, freely and with love—love that is the sacred and the ultimate energy of our universe. Together, we are our best resource. Feel free to take what you need and throw out the rest. Take care of yourself. You and your life are the most important.

Note: I am a sixty-ish cis-gendered, heterosexual, Caucasian female, and I have a life of privilege. I did my best to be sensitive to my unconscious biases. (We all have unconscious biases.) Anything I have written is not intended to offend. Please be generous and drop me a note at dralleyhay@gmail.com if I have offended you so I can check my biases.

Likewise, I am raised Christian and practice Buddhist principles. I believe in the Universe/God/the all of it. I believe that there have been great spiritual teachers among us walking the earth. I refer to "Father, Mother, God" in the prayers in the book as part of my patched together faith, realizing this is not the same for everyone. Your upbringing and journey are different and no less valid. Our commonality is the mystery and wonder of life. We see it every day as physicians.

Take care of you because you matter. You are not alone.

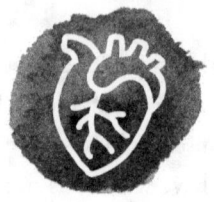

Have no fear of perfection; you'll never reach it.

—*Marie Curie*

On Perfection

What drives you? If you are someone addicted to work and busyness, you are probably addicted to perfection. We can't really become ourselves until we give up being perfect. Besides, as Madame Curie said, "You'll never reach it," so it is a self-perpetuating cycle.

If I am trying to be perfect and earn my worthiness and approval, I am doomed to always be on the hamster wheel of life. Besides, trying to look perfectly, act perfectly, perform perfectly, and live perfectly is exhausting. When we don't meet our mark of perfection, shame is lurking there to separate us from a vibrant life and our loved ones. Shame tells us that because we are not perfect, we're not worthy; we must earn love and acceptance.

Researchers also tell us that perfectionism limits success. Good-enoughness wins over perfection. We will fail, make mistakes, and disappoint others. Acceptance of imperfection is necessary to be human and experience life fully.

Today, I am worthy. I deserve love as I am. I don't have to strive so hard. I can let good-enoughness carry the day.

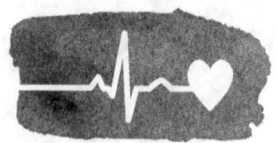

We are powerless over our busyness, and our lives have become unmanageable.

—*Modified Step One, Alcoholics Anonymous*

On First Steps

We women who do too much may be powerless over our addiction to work and busyness. Just like an alcoholic, the first step is admitting that there is a problem. Too many balls in the air at one time make it difficult to tend to things such as our own personal health, relationships, and mindful living. We can miss out on so much!

The question to ask is: What am I avoiding by all this busyness? What do I get out of my life being unmanageable?

These are difficult questions, so perhaps the first step is to look at our life from the outside of ourselves. What patterns do we see? What does it look like to be still? Can we be still?

Today I'll look for patterns of my busyness. What am I avoiding? What am I missing out on?

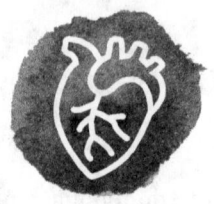

> To be fully seen by somebody, then, and be loved anyhow: This is a human offering that can border on miraculous.
>
> —*Elizabeth Gilbert*

On Acceptance

I learned acceptance when my mother was ill with Alzheimer's disease. I was stuck in grief at the loss of who I previously knew my mother to be, so much so that I wasn't present for the good times that were still possible. When I accepted my mother for all that she was and all that she was not, I had a whole new relationship with her. I was able to be present with her rather than in my grief, and we were able to make many new memories.

All I can control is myself, yet perhaps my mind or heart keeps forgetting that, and I want something "over there" to change about another person. I'm sorry, but the truth is it's not going to happen. To think it will is wishful thinking. What I do have is my ability to change—my ability to think and behave differently. That is really good news!

What would acceptance of people as the way they are and the way they are not look like? Rather than make the person or a situation wrong, we can bring generosity and acceptance. Then life is magical!

Today, I'll start building a magical life filled with generosity and acceptance—for the way things are and the way they are not.

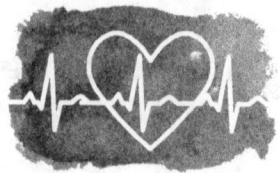

My tears break forth,
my will is overridden,

Reason retreats and
resolutions wane;

The stormy bursts of
weeping come
unbidden,

Wayward and fitful
as the April rain.

—*Makhfi*

On Crying

I think we don't like tears because we can't always control them, and they can sometimes make other people uncomfortable. What if we embraced our tears rather than resist them? Yes, they can be inconvenient when you have to wipe them away and blow your nose, especially when you don't have a hankie or a tissue. Yes, sometimes when we cry, we get that "ugly face" that is somewhat embarrassing and not our best look. And, it is certainly inconvenient when your mascara runs. But I have never understood the embarrassment and discomfort, except that it is all about looking good, perfect, and in control. We try so hard not to feel anything that will make us cry, and much of what we experience as physicians is worthy of tears. Thus, our need to be busy and outrun the tears

Perhaps today I will look at tears as prayers to God, thanksgiving and praise, and for forgiveness, and let them flow.

I carry within me
the heart of a warrior,
the mind of a pharaoh,
the soul of a goddess,
and the wisdom of
my grandmothers'
grandmothers."

—*Grace Gegenheimer*

On Our Ancestors

My women ancestors are real to me. I think we can learn a lot from them, as they provide answers and support, if you are willing to pause and hear them. I first came to know the ancient ones when I was in labor with my first child. Literally billions of women have labored and given birth over the millennium of human existence, yet when it was my turn to be in labor, I initially felt alone in the experience and was scared. Perhaps I was hallucinating from pain medicines and all the deep breathing, but once the ancestors showed up, all was calm and focus was the job at hand.

It was a bit like hearing women's soft voices saying, "We are here," and very old aunties simply present in the sacred circle they drew around me. The pain became sacred.

As an obstetrician, I've seen women go within during contractions. I've felt the sacred presence and space. They're there whenever we call. We are not alone. Ever.

Today, I will be open to my ancestors. If an ancient auntie showed up right now, what lessons would she bring?

Came to believe that a Power greater than ourselves could restore us to sanity.

—*Step Two, Alcoholics Anonymous*

On a Power Greater Than Ourselves

In 12-step programs for addiction, Alcoholics Anonymous encourage surrender to God or a power greater than ourselves as a basic tenet of the program to sobriety. We cannot do it alone.

We resist that surrender. Being in control is the basis of everything we try to do when we are martyring ourselves by doing too much. I want control, yet control keeps me stuck. It is an illusion of safety. Control was the glue that kept me together. It seemed like if I gave up the control, I would fall apart or dissolve like paper mâché in the rain. It is counter intuitive that giving up control could be a pathway to freedom from our busyness. This is why we must trust others who have been on the path to peace and freedom before us and surrender as a leap of faith.

If we hold onto control, we shrink ourselves and our lives. We feel stuck. It has an impact on ourselves and all the people in our lives.

Today, just for today, I'll take a leap of faith and trust in a Universal power/God/something bigger than myself. A joyful and expanded life for myself and my loved ones depends on it.

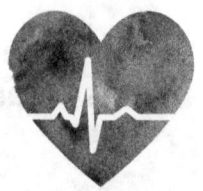

Bitterness is like cancer. It eats upon the host. But anger is like fire. It burns it all clean.

—*Maya Angelou*

On Anger

When we are overly concerned with the needs of others, our anger can get lost and come out in peculiar lashing-out bursts that have nothing to do with the real anger we carry. The anger is there, just hiding under the surface. Shhhh, don't wake it.

My anger manifests as depression and a lot of illness. What am I angry about? I am angry that in the past I was so busy that I lost myself. I am angry I didn't have more time with my children. I am angry I lost my marriage to busyness and regret. I am angry that I even have regrets. I am angry at myself. Oh, that's the part they talk about: anger turned inward.

I admit, I am still holding onto some of the anger. I keep working on it—to forgive others. To forgive myself. My anger has much to teach me about myself. "Slow down," she says. "Make amends. Bring compassion. Bring Spirit, dear one."

Dear anger, burn me clean.

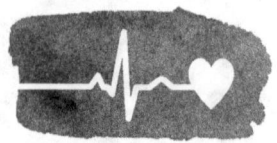

Once conform, once do what other people do because they do it, and a lethargy steals over all the finer nerves and faculties of the soul. She becomes all outer show and inward emptiness: dull, callous, and indifferent.

— *Virginia Woolf*

On Conformity

As physicians, we learn the "right" way. Over and over, we are given input (usually criticism, mostly direct, and maybe sharp or yelled) when we do something wrong. Yes, I have to do things right, the right diagnosis, the right treatment, the right dose, the right surgery, the right technique, the right interaction, the right care, even the right number of patients per day, per week, per month. Lives depend on us conforming.

We are taught to conform and make sure our colleagues and those that come after us conform. Well, what if I didn't conform? I am not saying that we don't do things the "right" way when it comes to medicine. I am saying that outside of our training and daily work, we can lose our uniqueness. And sooner or later we learn that life does not conform to the way we've been taught, planned, and accepted. That's okay. Life can be free flowing. Free. Flowing. I can be free flowing and unique.

Today, I'll remember that I am unique and deserve to let life flow freely.

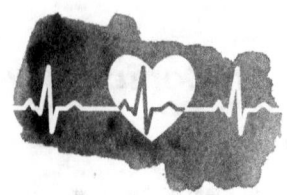

I felt like I was in a fog. I knew that I was desperately searching for something of great importance, the loss of which was life-threatening, but I couldn't see clearly.

—*Judy Ness*

On Awareness

Part of why we keep ourselves busy is because we are looking for something that we just can't quite make out with clarity. The fog is real. When we keep moving and moving, looking for perfection, a solution, what is missing, what we are really looking for is a sense of ourselves. In the busyness, we can lose her. We might feel like we are floating in this fog, or solidly on the ground in the thick of it, working exceedingly hard to move through it. It is exhausting.

How wonderful it is as we slow down and begin to let the fog lift.

Today, I will look within for myself.

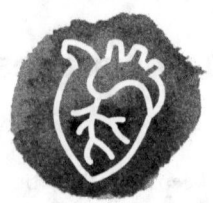

In our rushing, bulls in china shops, we break our own lives.

—*Ann Voskamp*

On Adrenaline

Mama docs know the adrenaline rush of a crisis. We live for the dopamine-driven high. Life becomes dramatic everywhere we look. We are superwomen—fast to fix every problem. The problem is that we have become trained, even addicted, to that high. The buzz of excitement, making a difference, saving a life, calmly leading a crisis, and rushing to the next activity eventually wears off. If we are honest with ourselves (which would require pausing to consider), it is taking a toll on our bodies and our psyches.

At some point, we begin to see that our rushes are leading to exhaustion and disruption to our lives. If we do our best under pressure, are we unsatisfied if everything is calm? Oh, what trouble we can find! Do we have difficulty being still? Are we inventing and inviting conflict at home because calm feels like a less-than life? We might be an average human being—oh no.

There is a fine line between the adrenaline rush and deep fulfillment in a job well done. This is a great inquiry and important place to know ourselves.

Today, I have discovered a place of peace and joy in the calm.

At the end of the day, darling, you are enough. You always have been. It may have taken you awhile to see that and to finally reach this place, but you have always been enough.

—*Lacey Ramburger*

On Getting Unstuck

Feeling like you are stuck at a point in life is not fun. We may be frozen in a stress state of disempowerment. There are three overall sympathomedullary reactions to stress: Fight, flight, and freeze. As a perfectionist, I get caught in freezing.

And guess what I do when I am frozen? I start listening to my negative thoughts. My predominant negative thought is, "I am not good enough." For me, this will rule my life—if I let it. If you are someone who does too much and are a recovering perfectionist, this is familiar to you, too.

Try this exercise: Write "I am good enough" on sticky notes and put them all over your house, car, office, desk, and bathroom mirror. Make sure you have one next to your bed so you see it first thing each morning.

Today, you are good enough. You've always been enough!

I want to get more comfortable being uncomfortable. I want to get more confident being uncertain.

—*Kristin Armstrong*

On Comfort

As physician leaders, we learn to be comfortable with the uncomfortable in clinical settings. When we are called on to step up in our performance or leadership, we are certainly uncomfortable, at first. It is the same for those you lead. We can learn to be comfortable with this discomfort. We can listen to ourselves and others as capable and competent—not as the discomfort of fear anxiety.

The anxiety will still be there, but so what? I can be in my discomfort when I compare it to my life purpose and vision. I have learned that my commitment to the physician clients I serve and the patients this will impact wins out over my discomfort. Every time. My commitment to my husband and our marriage wins out over the discomfort of an awkward or difficult conversation. Every time.

I see discomfort as a signal of growth and connection now.

Her breast and arms ached with the beauty of her own forgiveness.

—*Meridel Le Sueur*

On Forgiveness

If I tell myself the truth (and it is amazing how often we lie to ourselves), there are places of darkness of unforgiveness where can I be responsible—responsible for everything that has happened in my life, including the hurts, failures, and transgressions. [Note: This may be difficult for some who are truly victims of a perpetrator or past trauma. Please take care of yourself and work with a therapist, if needed.] We can't stay in victim-mode for too long or our life force oozes out of us. Through therapy and coaching, we can work to dissolve these dark areas and burdens to bring them into the light. Forgiveness of others and myself and taking responsibility where I can is all for myself and my own healing, not for anyone else.

Where can I work to let go of the hurt, the past, the baggage? Oh, how light I could be.

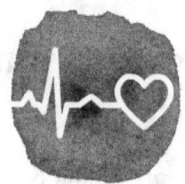

It is fact that everybody wants happiness and does not want suffering.

—*His Holiness the 14th Dalai Lama*

On Happiness

Everyone wants to be happy and there are many paths to happiness and a variety of ways to achieve happiness. In the same way, there are also myriad kinds and ways of suffering and a variety of ways to overcome the suffering.

Our good possessions like money, things, prestige, and power are all good—not wrong—but they are not real or permanent, thus our suffering. Developing the mind is eternal. Whether it is meditation only or part of a spiritual practice, we gain more lasting happiness through mental training that lasts and grows day by day.

Today, I'll start developing my mind and my spiritual practice. I'll remember that happiness and suffering are, in fact, temporary.

Comparison keeps you stuck in Fear Town. It will rob you of happiness and pure joy.

—*Melissa Ambrosini*

On Comparison

How many times a day do you compare yourself to others? It can be a constant, unrecognized, ongoing conversation in our heads. I know I am guilty every time I go on social media. Our lives look so small and untended when we compare them to the best moments of another person. We all tend to post our best moments. Chances are that if you are flipping through Facebook, you're not having one of your greatest moments at that time.

It is called "compare and despair."

Stop it.

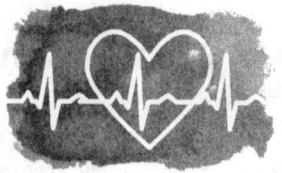

There is nothing enlightened about shrinking so that other people won't feel insecure around you.

—*Marianne Williamson*

On Badassness

Someone who mattered deeply to me once called me selfish. I can remember watching him forming the word. It has stuck with me for decades. I carried feelings of guilt, shame, and lack. Recently, it occurred to me that I was being called out as selfish when I was simply sure of myself and what I wanted. I took a stand for myself. That was not selfish. It was not a threat. I was simply a woman with confidence, power, and purpose.

Besides, when we are overly selfless, as most women in our culture tend to be, we end up truly being self less. We begin to lose our true selves. It does no good for the world to make ourselves small and underperform because someone might judge our power or feel threatened. That inner power is how we change the world.

Today, I give up guilt for being confident. I give up calling myself names such as "selfish." Perhaps I'll meet my badass self again.

If you want others to be happy, practice compassion. If you want to be happy, practice compassion.

—*His Holiness the 14th Dalai Lama*

On Compassion

First, to experience compassion for others, we have to recognize that they are suffering. Second, compassion is being moved by their suffering, and third, compassion is wanting to respond to their pain. Compassion literally means "to suffer with." When we feel another's pain and are moved by it, we are filled with caring, kindness, and the desire to help in some way. We do this without judgement. In those moments of compassion we realize that we all fail and are imperfect; it is our humanity showing. All of us experience failure, mistakes, losses, limitations, frustrations, and falling short. All of us deserve compassion because we are imperfect human beings in relationship with other imperfect human beings.

Just as having compassion for others, self-compassion involves recognizing our suffering and knowing we share that suffering with others in this world. Like compassion, there is no judgement in self-compassion (and no judgement if we do judge ourselves). Only kindness. There is no criticism or self-flagellation. Only kindness.

Today is for kindness to others and ourselves.

For me, the reason why people go to a mountaintop or go to the edge of the ocean is to look at something larger than themselves. That feeling of awe, of going to a cathedral, it's all about feeling lost in something bigger than oneself.

—*Diane Paulus*

On Awe

Have you ever laid in the grass and stared at the billowy clouds as they blow by, changing shape and form against the bright blue sky, the sun warming your skin like a warm bath? Or watched a thunderstorm roll in with its dark clouds, lightning, thunder, and curtains of rain? Maybe you've laid by the ocean in the warmth and silk of the sand, listening to the waves lap at the shore. Or breathed in the crisp and cool mountain air.

These are necessary delights for me. The sense of wonder and awe feed my soul—stop my busyness. The power and mystery of nature is food for the soul.

Today, I'll pause in nature to appreciate her beauty and power in a state of awe. I will allow myself to get lost—if only for a few precious moments.

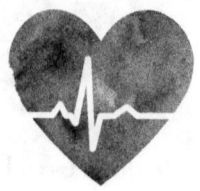

One loses many laughs by not laughing at oneself.

—*Sara Jeannette Duncan*

On Humor

At this point in my recovery, I get so much joy from laughing at myself. That sounds weird, but it is a sign of my recovery from perfectionism. I can appreciate to my soul how funny we can be as human beings. What other species has so many quirks and embarrassments. What other species actually experiences embarrassment, for that matter?

I had an elderly patient who I was seeing for early endometrial cancer. As I was getting ready to do her preoperative pelvic exam, I was on my usual gynecologist's perch (a swivel stool between her legs) putting on my gloves. The patient was scooting her bottom down to the proper position when I happened to notice, right at that moment, that her husband had brought fresh baked bread into the exam room with him. "That smells so good!" I exclaimed, not thinking of where I was! My elderly patient sat bolt upright and exclaimed "What? I smell good?!" Oh, my gosh, I was so embarrassed that I said something so stupid at an inopportune and inappropriate time and place! Luckily, we all had a good laugh. She did well with her surgery, and the couple continued to drop by to bring us fresh bread, always with a laugh.

I am a great source of humor. Aren't we funny as human beings?

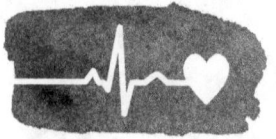

I'm so tired that my bones ache.

—Anonymous

On Exhaustion

Keeping up with society's demands, our careers, and our families in patriarchal, hierarchical systems is exhausting. How often do we feel like a pretzel trying to mold into what is expected, doing more, working harder, and striving for perfection? It is exhausting! It is like Sisyphus pushing the boulder up the hill—only to have it roll back down. It takes enormous quantities of energy to be how we are not.

Exhaustion may be a sign of my striving to fit in, be better, be best, or prove myself. I recognize this has made me sick. I have created a habit of perfectionism and a too busy life. "Work harder and longer" has been my mantra up to this day.

Today, I'll chose a different mantra: "I am enough."

Do one thing every day that scares you. Those small things that make us uncomfortable help us build courage to do the work we do.

—*Eleanor Roosevelt*

On Being Uncomfortable

We can learn to get comfortable with the uncomfortable. It is a skill to be practiced. Really.

Faced with starting a women's cancer screening program at 12,000 feet in the Himalayas was daunting. I had no idea how I was going to do it. I had my equipment that I prayed would make the bumpy two-day drive through the mountains on barely passible roads. I was uncomfortable in the unknown. I was physically uncomfortable in a vehicle bouncing along cliffs with seven cramped souls banging into each other for 20 hours. I used to be claustrophobic. I used to have a bit of social anxiety. I used to.

What kept me sane during that trip? It was my commitment to our medical mission and the wonderful Tibetan Buddhist people we would serve. Why do we put ourselves through medical school and learning life-and-death procedures? Because of our commitment to serve.

It is a practice to breathe and visualize the outcome of our commitment. Breathe, dear friends.

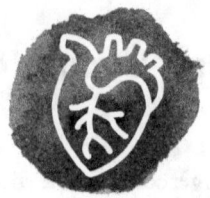

In practicing meditation, we're not trying to live up to some kind of ideal—quite the opposite. We're just being with our experience, whatever it is.

—*Pema Chödrön*

On Beginning Meditation

Beginning to meditate can seem daunting (at least it did for me). We think the goal is to get to a focused place of nothing without distraction. Many too busy professionals are used to being able to do something perfect and become frustrated early on because their mind continually drifts. This is what the mind does; it is normal!

It may be more helpful to simply become aware of when the mind drifts sooner every time we meditate and be able to bring awareness back to the breath or other focus with nonjudgement of the self. Practicing nonjudgement of oneself is a great goal and a very useful step for recovery.

Today, my goal is to sit in silence, focusing on my breath and letting go of doing it right for at least three minutes. My mind will wander, and I can gently refocus my thoughts without judgement.

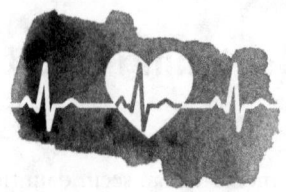

Your perception of me, of life, of others ... is always a reflection of something in you.

—*Brittany Burgunder*

On Perception

One day, my husband and I entered a hospital. I, as a doctor, noticed the people and familiar sights. He, as a builder, spotted nothing about the people, but commented on the layout of the hospital and the trim details of the walls. We marveled at how differently we experienced the same five-minute walk through the hospital! Could we really be experiencing the same reality?

We all have a way of seeing the world—our tinted glasses, so to speak. Sometimes, we have them on so long that we no longer see that they are tinted. We have it that what we see is real and the truth. How often do we stop to consider the color of our glasses or the glasses of another? I forget that I see pink with my pink tinted glasses, and your glasses may be tinted a different color, like blue. There is nothing and no one that is wrong—just different.

If we can learn to consider the viewpoint of others and get curious, we open a whole new world for ourselves. Wow, the arguments that can be saved.

Today, I'll try changing glasses just for fun!

Pity those who don't feel anything at all.

—*Sarah J. Maas*

On Emotions

I used to expect people around me to guess and interpret my feelings. How unfair! I was not adept at feeling and expressing them in the first place. Prior to being a recovering busyoholic, I had not heard of emotional intelligence. It turns out that we all have an emotional vocabulary. Mine was just limited.

How is your emotional vocabulary? I may say I'm angry, but if I have a large emotional library, I can express myself more pointedly. My anger might really be hostility, frustration, or disappointment.

Emotions are feelings from a five year old! By increasing our emotional vocabulary, we can pinpoint an emotion and thereby acknowledge it with consciousness. If I can name it, I can normalize it. If I normalize it, I can let it go and make decisions from a place where I am free to choose.

The goal is not to hide from your feelings or sublimate them, but to label and express them. By being honest with ourselves and our loved ones about how we're feeling, we can move on to conscious choice in the matter.

Today, I'll ask: What am I really feeling?

Forgiveness is not always easy.
At times, it feels more painful than
the wound we suffered, to forgive
the one that inflicted it.
And yet, there is no peace
without forgiveness.

—*Marianne Williamson*

On Forgiveness

To truly transform ourselves and have the kind of lives we want, we must look at the impact of the unforgiveness we're holding onto. Unforgiveness is sneaky in that it weighs us down, and we don't even realize it.

The forgiveness I am talking about is about putting the relationship as be-fore – as in "I forgive you (the situation, the event, the person, ourselves) and will not hold it against you ever again."

To hold onto it means a heaviness or like dragging suitcases of the past with us into the future. Do you want to set it down to feel lighter? If not, consider the impact on you not putting the suitcases down.

Today, I'll look to see what weight I am carrying. Perhaps forgiveness is possible, and I can unpack a suitcase.

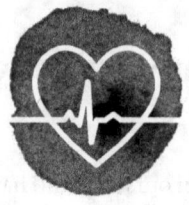

Lack of integrity messes with my life and my opinion of myself.

—*Robyn Alley-Hay*

On Integrity

From Webster's Dictionary:
Integrity – 1. the quality of being honest and having strong moral principles; moral uprightness. 2. the state of being whole and undivided

Most of us have been taught that integrity is about right and wrong. If I have integrity, I'll do things the right and moral way. What if integrity is the second definition "the state of being whole and undivided"? What would it look like if I were whole? Am I whole right now? Certainly, being too busy and doing too much divides me so I don't feel whole.

A bicycle wheel must have all of its spokes, or it is weakened and impacts performance of the rider. What spokes am I missing?

Perhaps it is my body that is out of integrity with those extra pounds. Perhaps it is my car that needs that oil changed. Or, like my car, has a window that won't operate. Perhaps it is my word: my promise to call someone that I haven't called and am now embarrassed to call. It may be my angry words that I know I should not have said and have not apologized for. Each one of these examples chips away at our wholeness and peace of mind.

Today, I am taking an integrity survey.

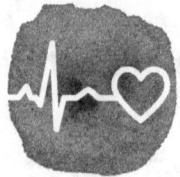

So, whatever you want to do, just do it. Making a damn fool of yourself is absolutely essential.

—*Gloria Steinem*

On Failure

Trying to be perfect and avoid failing is part of the addiction to doing too much. "Making a damn fool of yourself is absolutely essential" sounds like pure torture to me, or at least it did at first. As I paused and found what I had lost in the process of burnout, like a sense of purpose and passion, I had to be willing to be a damn fool. I had to be willing to fail. After making this shift, my thoughts are no longer self-directed trying to fix myself, rather they are directed at what is important to me. To make an impact in the world requires the willingness to be a fool that can fail and be less than perfect. And I will fail if my purpose in life is large enough.

Today, I will fail at something on purpose! Perhaps I'll doodle a picture or burn my partner's toast. What a foolish thing to do!

Don't be confused between who people say you are and who you know you are.

—*Oprah Winfrey*

On Self-Worth

Are you grounded in your own self-worth? Confident that you are enough? Appreciate your past failings and wisdom gained? Sought to nourish your soul and grow?

Things that get in the way of being unmesswithable:
People pleasing
Looking good
Perfectionism
Workaholism
Need for approval
Stuck on past failings
Lack of forgiveness and generosity

Any of these ring true? Then you are messwithable! We all have some of these tendencies, but the unmesswithable do not need them.

Recovery involves knowing and being myself without the need to be anything or anyone else. I am willing to be myself today.

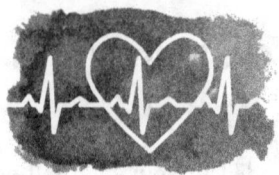

Treasure yourself for being, not doing.

—*Gina Greenlee*

On Being versus Doing

As we recover from our too-busyness, we find the freedom to just be. We know doing, doing, doing, but can we simply be? Can we simply be good enough in a single moment?

When I first decided to slow down the doing, doing, doing, I didn't really know who I could "be." It has been delightful to get to know myself and have many more moments of being. I simply be.

Today, ask yourself who is doing the being?

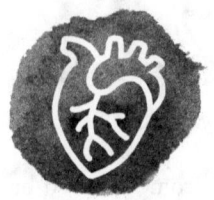

When one is a stranger to oneself, then one is estranged from others too.

—*Ann Wilson Schaaf*

On Estrangement

Do you ever feel like you're a stranger to yourself? Have you kept yourself busy enough to forget who you are?

In my first marriage I forgot who I was. I blamed him for my emptiness, of course, but it was actually my busy me—the busy me not willing to get to know herself. What if I looked and didn't like what I found? So, I just didn't look. I looked outward to others to tell me who I was. Blaming others is much easier than looking at the emptiness within. Of course, my husband and I became estranged.

If you don't know yourself and all you know is doing, life rolls by like a train that you never bought a ticket for. You forget where you were going.

Today, I'll take the first step to knowing myself: I'll slow down.

There are in life a few moments so beautiful that even words are a sort of profanity.

—*Diana Palmer*

On Awe

When my children were little, we would take a "hike" in the woods. We never got very far! There was seeing the awesome, right there in a step's worth of ground, earth, foliage, insects, clouds, and sky. Children have a sense of awe that we sometimes forget. I can remember standing at the bottom of the Grand Canyon, feeling as small as a grain of sand from the sandstone cliffs. We really are a tiny spec in the firmament of the Universe, yet at the same time we have a whole Universe within.

We can create moments to be in awe and experience moments of meditative expansiveness if we remember to look at the small details: the present moment in time in just one footstep.

I only have to look around to discover awe and whole Universes of life.

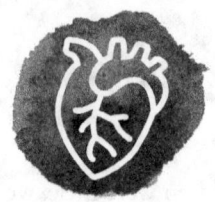

The passion for setting people right is in itself an afflictive disease.

—*Marianne Williamson*

On Arrogance

I used to think arrogance lived in the patriarchal narcissists in medicine I would meet. After all, in my experience, many are braggadocios. Little did I know that arrogance would reside in me.

As women physicians who are driven and striving for excellence, we know a lot, a lot, a lot. We have seen life and death. We have held it in our hands and laid it to rest. But being an expert is one thing; we are experts on the human body, illness and wellness, but we think we are the expert in the lives of our patients (and our spouses, children, friends, family). We can tend to judge them as right or wrong, or needing fixing and tell them what to do, rather than partner with them.

Actually, our patients are the experts of their own lives. Just because we know a lot doesn't mean we know a thing about what is best for them (or our spouses, children, friends, family). The assumption that we do is arrogance.

Today, I will check my arrogance at the door: the patient room door, the door to my house, and all the other doors I open for friends and family.

If you haven't forgiven yourself something, how can you forgive others?

—*Dolores Huerta*

On Forgiveness

Empiric evidence shows that forgiveness benefits physical health, mental health, relationships, and personal spirituality. We've known this for almost three decades. So, why is it so hard to forgive others and even harder to forgive ourselves?

We carry non-forgiveness in our bodies and souls. It's heavy. Maybe it is time to put it down, especially because the one doing the forgiving benefits the most.

Today, who can I forgive? What do I need to forgive myself for? Can I put it down?

Meditations for Women Physicians (and Others) Who Do Too Much

PRAYER

Father, Mother, God, grant me the ability:

To see when I am grasping and doing, rather than being in your love,

To remove the obstacles in my life that keep me stuck and separate from you,

To see the illusion of control and her seductive ways,

To nourish my soul on behalf of others.

To remove obstacles to right thinking and presence, so, in my life, I dwell in you.

Amen

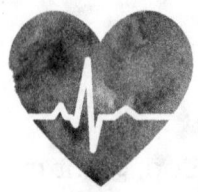

What I am actually saying is that we each need to let our intuition guide us and then be willing to follow that guidance directly and fearlessly.

—*Carolyn Myss*

On Intuition

What is intuition, really? Neuroscientists say intuition is simply shortcuts in the brain and neural networks of the heart and gut. We sense observations with the heightened instincts, sight, hearing, smell, taste, and feel before they reach our logical brain. There is a reason our children think their mothers have eyes in back of their head!

In western allopathic medicine, we do not value intuition as a diagnostic tool per se, but I suspect we use it a lot more than is recognized. I have sensed things with patients that didn't make any sense, and I would not have made a diagnosis otherwise. How many times have you walked into a room and sensed tension or sadness before you even got halfway into the exam room? How many times has a still, small voice told you to check that liver panel or other diagnostic test? Our intuition can serve us.

Today, I choose to use my intuition. I will honor my own still, inner voice.

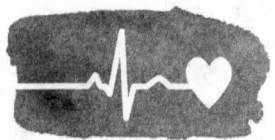

Over-working gets less done. We all have experienced this. We can push ourselves to exhaustion, but things get done with less attention, and our bodies eventually break down.

—*Tara Stiles*

On Exhaustion

I'm exhausted. Don't you see?

Keeping up with society's demands and male hierarchical systems is exhausting. Being in a male-oriented world makes it hard to be our true selves. Sometimes we lose ourselves entirely. How often do we either take it out on ourselves, or become more masculine and inauthentic just to survive? We wonder, "Why don't they see how exhausted I am?"

Living in a masculine world, it is important to know our Goddess gifts, for the exhaustion comes from continuing the charade of being who we are not. It is exhausting participating in systems that we know do not work. It hurts our feminine and wise woman souls.

I have learned my Goddess gifts. I powerfully claim them. I am tired of pretending.

A girl should be two things: who and what she wants.

—*Coco Chanel*

On Being Unmesswithable

When you are unmesswithable (some would call this unf*ckwithable), you know who you are, what you stand for, and what is important to you. You are at peace. Nothing can shake you, and negativity does not touch you. So, if we are busy doing all the time, do we know ourselves deeply?

Being too-busy physicians (myself included), many of us haven't matured on a psyche/self level or done a very good job nourishing our soul for the needed growth of life. Yes, life can be lived superficially. We go to work, come home, have superficial conversations, offer perfunctory kisses for the kids and partner, sleep, and repeat. Life events can really mess with people who do not develop soul skills and deep experiences to meet the challenges of life.

How well have you gotten to know and develop your self and soul? When you are unmesswithable, life has room for joy and contentment.

Today, I'll do at least one thing to nourish my soul.

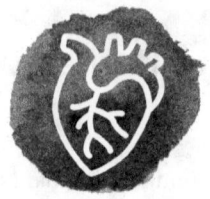

The season is changeable, fitful, and maddening as I myself these days that are cloaked with too many demands and engagements.

—*Mary Sarton*

On Busyness

I can remember being so busy with my practice and four growing kids that I thought I was going to go crazy. I was exhausted and not so nice to be around sometimes.

Being too busy and overextended causes drama for ourselves and the ones we love. We are irritable, change moods all over the place, and take it out on anyone nearby—all while thinking, "Doesn't anyone see how busy I am? I'm dying here."

Putting the responsibility of making the time we need on others is not fair and causes a lot of drama and crises. It is my responsibility to voice my needs. Just like a surgical nurse can't read my mind to hand me the right instrument, if we don't ask "scalpel… retractor…, Kelly," we can't expect others to tend to our need.

Today, I will survey my own needs and be in communication about them. Life can be without drama.

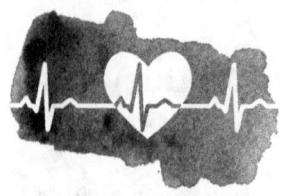

You are your own worst enemy. If you can learn to stop expecting impossible perfection, in yourself and others, you may find the happiness that has always eluded you.

—*Lisa Kleypas*

On Expectations

Expectations—what a loaded word! In my marriage, I had a certain picture in my mind of how it was supposed to go. When the reality did not live up to the expectation, I was disappointed and angry. Not only did I expect perfection from myself, but I expected perfection from my spouse. There was a "right" way things should go. I got to be superior to him because he was obviously wrong. I was right. He failed me over and over when reality didn't fit my expectations.

Unreasonable expectations are a way to control and hide in disappointment: to be let down, yet again, to demand unhealthy perfection from ourselves, and expectation that others be perfect as well. Where is the acceptance and joy in that?

I have learned that I can give up unreasonable expectations of myself and others. I am ready to let others breathe freely. Right now, I can breathe in freedom and gratitude and let go of controlling others.

... I learned that true forgiveness includes total acceptance. And out of acceptance, wounds are healed and happiness is possible again.

—*Catherine Marshall*

On Forgiveness

One of the first steps to forgiveness is a commitment to forgive. This sounds like a simple task, but let's step back a bit. We have to know where we are holding onto negative feelings about a person or ourselves. This is hard work and definitely not for everyone. But the freedom on the other side of forgiveness is sweet! Forgiveness is like cleaning your closet, removing clutter, or shedding pounds. It clears out a space for us to thrive, create, and even focus better. If you're not ready to commit to forgiveness, that's okay, too. Be gentle with yourself first and foremost.

Today, I remind myself to be gentle to myself and bring love to those areas that are dark and nasty. It's okay.

Dearest Muchkins: don't unmuch yourself. MAYBE IT'S THEM.

—*Glennon Doyle*

On Muchness

Do you ever feel like you've lost your "muchness"? And what does muchness look like?

In the middle of my career, I knew my muchness was disappearing. How could I keep up? How could I work harder, better, best? How did I lose my "muchness"? Burnout. Burnout that led to depression and a suicide scare. My journey to recovery was very much all about finding my muchness after unmuching myself to please others.

Muchness is our spark, our highest self, the inner self that is expansive, our vitality of life. When I lost my muchness, life became heavy. Lightness of being and authentic expression is our native state. What did you like to do when you were younger? Where did that playful being go? Yes, there is what we do to live, to work, to love for that is life, but we can choose to dress the mundane and familiar in all kinds of color. My muchness is bright and outrageous and fun—still there.

Your muchness is there for you, too.

ON MINI MEDITATIONS

Many people have a difficult time beginning a regular meditation practice and then maintaining it. If you are one of those people, perhaps these mini meditations will help you bring mindfulness to your day. Start with just one to three minutes the same time each day.

1. Do one mindful breath when you think about it. On the inbreath, feel the air fill your lungs to the count of 4. Pause for a count of 4 and breath out to a count of 4, paying attention to a soft belly and air flowing over your lips, pause to a count of 4. Repeat.

2. Do the same as #1 only through the nose. Concentrate on the temperature change on the skin below your nose with each inbreath and outbreath.

3. Take a long deep breath, noticing any sensations or tightness in your body and try to soften anywhere you are tense on the outbreath.

4. Rub two fingers together lightly with such attention that you can feel the ridges of your fingertips.

5. Sit with your feet flat on the floor and imagine outlining your foot—like you might have done as with crayons as a child.

6. Sit and listen to sounds farthest away and then switch to sounds closest to you.

7. Stare out the window, focusing on an object or a scene, and pause for a minute in your day. If you're in a windowless room, the same can be done with objects in the room.

8. Take a mindful walk, noticing your feet as they touch the ground with each step. Notice the scenery overall and then in minute detail. Notice the sun's warmth or the air on your exposed skin and breathe!

9. Make up your own mini-meditation and make it a habit.

These are borrowed from many different sources over the years. I know I started my meditation practice this way, with tiny little moments daily.

Today, I'll give up the all-or-none thinking I have had about meditation. I have as many ways to meditate as I can think of.

Life shrinks or expands in proportion to one's courage.

—Anais Nin

On Courage

Physical courage is the knight in shining armor saving the princess, or a mother finding super strength and ability to protect a child from harm, putting her own life at risk. This kind of courage is celebrated in our culture.

Researchers say that courage is actually a process, not an accolade. As a process, courage is: 1) an intentional act, 2) taken after mindful contemplation, 3) involves taking considered risk, 4) motivated by a worthy and/or a desirable result, 5) taken in spite of emotional fear.

We exhibit courage in our lives daily. Social courage is when we speak up or speak out in relationships or groups. Moral courage is standing up for what is right in the face of resistance by others. Emotional courage is moving away from our negative thoughts. Giving up destructive behaviors takes courage. Every time we are willing to face judgement, we are being courageous.

Today, acknowledge yourself with each courageous act. If it is a process, then it can become a practice. Who knows where you will go!

Meditations for Women Physicians (and Others) Who Do Too Much

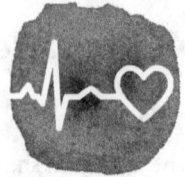

The more of me I be, the clearer I can see.

—*Rachel Andrews*

On Clarity

When we are addicted to doing too much, we can avoid getting clear because if we really brought clarity to our lives, then we might have a clear view of what needs to change. There might be decisions that we may need to make, relationships to leave, activities to cancel, or difficult conversations to have. Fuzziness or confusion are forms of resistance to looking at these situations and relationships. Rather than clarity, we hold on to that niggly feeling of incompletion and overwhelm. We're stuck and seemingly confused.

The first step is to admit to ourselves that we have a problem with doing too much. Our lives have become out of our control and unmanageable by our own making. Take the first step, and then you can begin the search for clarity and thus make room for joy and fun!

Today, I'll look at one area of my life that needs clarity. What am I resisting?

Service rests on the basic premise that the nature of life is sacred, that life is a holy mystery, which has an unknown purpose. When we serve, we know that we belong to life and to that purpose. When you help, you see life as weak. When you fix, you see life as broken. When you serve, you see life as whole.

—*Dr. Rachel Remen*

On Fixing People

As busy people, we are darn good at fixing—fixing things, fixing people, fixing situations. As physicians, that is what we are doing a lot of the time with patients—forgetting to serve and automatically switching into "fix it" mode. The worst part about that is that we continue to 'fix it' when we go home. It's part of being too busy: Fix this, fix that with the wave of our magic wand!

Stop fixing! When I consciously gave up fixing people, places, and things, I found so much freedom and peace on the other side. And it allowed me to be of service as a whole person who is not broken, just like my patients, my loved ones, and situations are not broken. To do otherwise is to manipulate and control, which is part of our dis-ease.

Today, I'll look for where I am fixing, whether of good intentions or a need to control others.

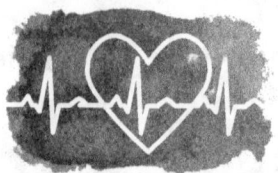

There is no greater gift you can give or receive than to honor your calling. It's why you were born. And how you become most truly alive.

—*Oprah Winfrey*

On Purpose

Do you have a "big ass why"?

What are you committed to?

What breaks your heart?

What are you passionate about?

These questions help find your "big ass why" you became a doctor (or whatever profession you might work in). "Why" becomes the touchstone in life. When we know our "why," the day-to-day annoyances don't bring us down. Instead, life is joy and fulfillment.

My purpose in my career as an Ob/Gyn was to work toward a world of safety and love for all mothers and babies. I cared for mothers, aunties, daughters, and families in service to this "why." Later, I worked on a project with the Dalai Lama to bring Western medicine to a population of Tibetan Buddhist midwives. Now, I coach the physicians that care for the mothers and babies—all a part of my "why."

Today, I will explore my possible "big ass why". What makes my heart sing about the work I do? What am I committed to? What breaks my heart? What am I passionate about?

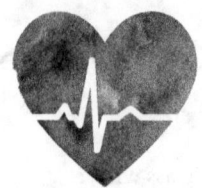

You can be a good person with a kind heart and still say no.

–*Lori Deschene*

On Saying "No"

Do you have trouble saying "no"? Do you feel guilty when you do say "no"? I am a total people pleaser. "No" used to be difficult and when I did say "no", I'd leave the conversation feeling that tinge of guilt and self-reproach for not saying "yes."

A powerful way to say "no" is to take a moment, listen to what is being asked carefully so the person asking feels heard, and then consciously decide if it works for you or not. Reframing requests to workability (rather than right/wrong) can give us another way to look at the request. Is it workable? (And, by the way, asking yourself "What do I want to do?" is part of workability.) Then, the answer is matter of fact. "No, I am sorry, that doesn't work for me at this time." Or, "Let me look at my calendar to see if that works." Or, "No, thank you for asking."

And remember "no" can be a full sentence!

Today, I'll begin to look at workability of the requests of me. I have a choice to say "no"!

I'm obsessed with being human.

—*Rachelle Lefevre*

On Being Human

What would it be like to stop thinking of ourselves as either good or bad? Perhaps if we gave up this rigid thinking, we could accept ourselves as neither good or bad and simply accept ourselves with loving kindness. We are flawed human beings in relationship to other flawed human beings. This is the nature of life. How nice it would be to put down the perfectionism that leads to overworking and busyness to just be, well, human.

Today, I'll treat myself with loving kindness and realize that I am a flawed human being in relationship to other flawed human beings. That is life!

True courage is about facing life without flinching. I don't mean the times when the right path is hard, but glorious at the end. I'm talking about enduring the boredom, the messiness, and the inconvenience of doing what is right.

—*Robin Hobb*

On Everyday Courage

Yes, we can have courage in the face of our fears. Yes, we can be good at taking risks and conquering fear. But that is not the same as everyday courage.

Do we have the courage for daily life? Do we have the courage to be ourselves? Are we courageous enough to have the difficult conversations with a colleague or at home with our spouse? Do we have the courage to say "no" as a full sentence?

Ask these questions: Where am I not giving myself enough credit for my everyday courageous self? Where am I pretending it doesn't matter? Do you say to yourself: "I don't want to be seen as the courageous woman I am?" Am I taking responsibility for my courageous power? Does that scare me? Who am I when I experience that power?

I have found courage as a way of being. I am courageous in life every day.

Now is the time to be responsible for my own power.

Today, I am courage.

The art of life is not controlling what happens to us but using what happens to us.

—*Gloria Steinem*

On Control

Control and perfectionism go hand in hand. There is an illusion that we can control life, situations, environments, and people. To some extent as a doctor, we are in charge and expected to be in control of a situation. The problem is that we can use control to dominate. I am used to being in charge in the OR, but it doesn't work so well when I try it with family and friends!

When we stop to remember that we really are not in charge of anything, except ourselves and our choices in the moment, life gets lighter and we feel lighter. In that way, we can make room for Grace—for ourselves and our imperfections and for others who are doing their best. We can experience this moment for the highest and best good of all.

Where have we been resisting letting go of control? Where can we surrender that control in favor of putting our experience to good use?

Today, I'll surrender control in favor of Grace and see what happens.

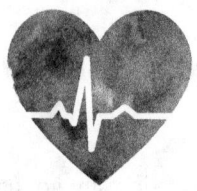

Certainly, tears are given to us to use. Like all good gifts, they should be used properly.

—*Loretta Young*

On Tears

Tears are a mixed bag for most women. Are we supposed to cry or not cry? Crying in front of the boss or a patient is a big no, no. Why are women perceived as weak when there are tears? We have tears of anger, frustration, sadness, fear. There are also tears of happiness, joy, and awe. We have tears, too, when dust is in our eyes or we eat hot pepper in a delicious meal. We cry tears before God, tears in childhood when we are hurt or scared and our mothers kissed them away, delicious tears with our lover when we touch another so deeply that you see God, tears of profound gratitude when someone goes out of their way for us, and tears in childbirth with pain and joy all mixed together.

When I look at this list of times and circumstances of tears, I do not see anything but powerful moments as part of being alive—as humans.

What if we welcomed tears as receptiveness to life?

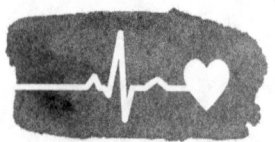

To say that a person feels listened to means a lot more than just their ideas get heard. It's a sign of respect. It makes people feel valued.

—*Deborah Tannen*

On Listening

If you want some magic in your life, listen for what people are committed to and what they want to be acknowledged for. When we can get, I mean really get, someone's communication and the commitments they speak from, we are listening beyond the words. We must get curious and be open-minded to hear people's truth and what is important to them.

One day, my daughter called in tears after starting her first job. "My boss doesn't care about me, the job, or the clients. Is this what all jobs are like?" She asked for my coaching. As I listened, I could hear my daughter's commitment to find a possible solution. As an exercise, I asked her to listen to her boss with curiosity and an open mind and to make her look good for her boss—and do this for three days. It turns out her boss was really struggling with nausea of pregnancy and could really use my daughter's assistance to do a good job. My daughter could get behind her to get the work done. It changed the tenor of the whole office! Of course, I was proud of my daughter, but more importantly, she learned a new listening skill that was powerful enough to change lives. (And I didn't have to tell her that her boss sucks, which was my first thought.)

Today, I'll be present and curious in every conversation I have.

Why indeed must "God" be a noun?
Why not a verb—the most active
and dynamic of all?

—*Mary Daly*

On Belief

I sometimes have trouble with the word "God." I tend to think of God as early Christians have portrayed: as a him, father, lord, judgement in the sky. But God was also Jesus on earth. I can relate to Jesus. He was a man in process. He lived, he loved, he suffered. He was of man, not of perfection.

I look at my life as being in process. I am in-process of being my authentic and loving self, rather than who others think I should be or could be. I seek oneness with divine process.

Today, as a child of God, I seek oneness with my authentic and loving being in-process: my Self.

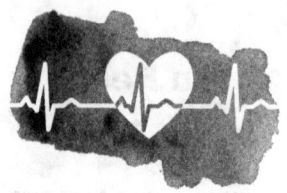

I swing between procrastination
and being really thorough
so either way things aren't
getting done quickly.

—*Freema Agyeman*

On Perfectionism and Procrastination

Workaholic perfectionists often feel stuck in procrastination; it's the effect of being a woman who is doing too much. We are doing too much to the point of exhaustion and either drop to the sofa or have a desire to numb ourselves with the tv, social media, or booze. There are things to be done, but we have pushed to our limits. And then, of course, the items on the to-do list pile up. Then, when we do get around to our list, we find the perfectionist has to be meticulous about the simplest things and nothing gets done.

Why do workaholism and perfectionism go together? For myself, I was always trying to have the perfect life and reach the unreachable standards I set for myself. Doing any chore, or even fun activity, became laborious and exhausting. Thus, the cycle: work too much, feel exhausted, procrastinate, finally do something, have to do it perfectly, become exhausted and behind again. Go to bed and repeat the cycle in the morning.

Wow. That is not having joy and fulfillment!

Today, good enough is done. I am committed to breaking the cycle.

What a relief it is to admit our fears! What a relief it is to admit that we are powerless over our fears and they are making our life unmanageable!

—*Anne Wilson Schaef*

On Fear

Fears are meant to be helpful and protective. The next time I run into a saber-toothed tiger, I'll appreciate it. Mostly, fear keeps me from doing really cool stuff in my life, and I use it to keep me safe. Right now, I am putting together a video coaching course, and fear has me frozen. I go home to my husband, and I am not sure I am going to bring up a topic I need to discuss because I'm afraid he'll not love me. I don't do networking events; they occur to me as being eaten by that tiger.

Having all of these fears keeps me safe—really safe, like limited to a contracted life safe. But once I give up those fears to a higher power, there is a space to take a breath, thank the fear for protecting me, and leave it to God.

Today, I will admit my powerlessness over my fears. Maybe there is space to talk to God.

Superwoman syndrome: a set of characteristics found in a woman who performs or attempts to perform all the duties typically associated with several different full-time roles, such as wage earner, mother, homemaker, and wife.

—*APA Dictionary of Psychology*

On Delegating

Do you have Superwoman Syndrome? I had no idea this was a real thing. I think every woman physician is a superwoman to begin with. We have made sacrifices for the long hours of medical school and residency/fellowship training. It is not unusual to work 80 hours or more a week, and we accept this as normal. And surprise! It is not sustainable.

Rather than doing everything ourselves, learning to delegate can literally save a career, a marriage, and personal sanity. I remember a male colleague telling me he had to leave work early because he was "babysitting" his kids! What the actual f? No one is going to see our suffering. We must recognize it for ourselves and off-load the less pressing chores and duties. My husband may not load the dishwasher the same way that I do, but it is good enough. It is not failure to acknowledge that you need help. It is smart.

Today, I'll be smart. I'll look at my tasks and ask for good enough help.

> Listening is an attitude of the heart, a genuine desire to be with another, which both attracts and heals.
>
> —*L. J. Isham*

On Listening Skills

Listening skills are probably the most useful, timesaving, and life-fulfilling skills there are. This does not mean listening to the first sentence and assuming the rest. This means sitting with a person until they have communicated what there is for them—until they have said all there is to say about the topic.

For doctors, this does not mean thinking of the patient diagnosis and plan while the patient is speaking. It is tempting to think it saves time, but does it really?

Presence is the number one skill.

Second is listening for the content of what is being said.

Third is listening for the feeling/emotional state behind what is being said.

Fourth is listening for the needs being expressed under the feelings.

And lastly, listening for the person's commitment (what is important to them) behind all of that.

Whew! That sound like a lot! It is a lot. This takes practice.

Today, I will start by setting aside my thoughts while another is speaking to me and listen with presence and generosity.

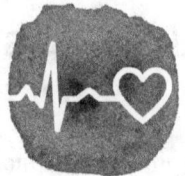

I am as my Creator made me, and since He [sic] is satisfied, so am I.

—*Minnie Smith*

On Goddess

Who are we to belittle what our Creator has made? It could be thought of as arrogance to put our Self down or harshly criticize who we are. Who are we to compare our perfect form and being to an unreachable beauty standard? Who are we to compare our lives to some vision of an unrealistic "perfect" life? It is the opposite of humility.

If I am humble, I am accepting of myself as whole and perfect, just the way I am and the way I am not. It is only then that we can appreciate the perfection of our world the way it is and is not. We are fashioned as Goddesses by our Creator. We are reflections of God. Who are we to mess with that?

Today, I'll try on thinking of my Self as whole, perfect, and complete. The way I am and the way I am not. That's humility.

"Go away," she said to the guilt. Guilt wanted her most when she least wanted it.

—*Ann Brashares*

On Guilt

For a long time, as a business owner, I believed that if I was not constantly working on my coaching business, then my business wasn't working. I felt guilty. "Work harder and longer" was my mantra, and anything less than arduous felt like I wasn't giving my business the time and attention it needed to be successful.

I had to face guilt head on. First of all, guilt is a feeling associated with a collection of thoughts and body sensations. The feeling doesn't have to mean anything: It means what I say it means. Second, it is not action oriented; it doesn't help you accomplish anything. Often, when we experience guilt and do not examine it, we are more likely to be reactive than to make decisions based on facts and honest reflection. Guilt feeds self-doubt and negativity and blocks open, creative, productive thinking.

Today, I can examine guilt as a feeling, with associated thoughts and body sensations that I assign meaning to. Ultimately, it doesn't help me accomplish what I wish to accomplish in the world.

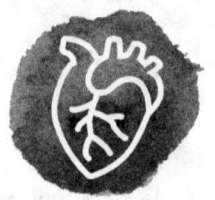

Find a happy person, and you will find a project.

—*Sonja Lyubomirsky*

On Projects

I love this quote because we are all projects in process. It is when we forget to be in-process that we forget to be happy. I believe that our lives are not about arriving at happiness but moving beyond happiness to feeling all our emotions.

Today, I'll consider myself a project in process.

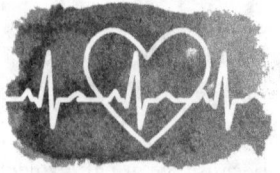

Document the moments you feel most in love with yourself: what you're wearing, who you're around, what you're doing. Recreate and repeat.

—*Warsan Shire*

On Self-Love

I love this quote. We all have an inner self-critic that will tell us that we're not good enough. Physiologically, the brain is skewed to the negative. It helped our ancestors survive for thousands of years, and it never shuts up. It takes practice to calm that critic and love yourself.

For most of my life, being in love with myself was a foreign concept. I continue to work on self-love, as that love will grow with practice.

How about you? Can you fall in love with yourself? Can you love yourself in your imperfections? The invitation is to say "thank you, no" to the inner critic, or at least turn down the volume and bring awareness.

Today, I love me! Take some "me time" to foster the relationship!

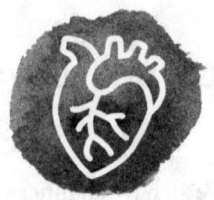

The critical voices in our own heads are far more vicious than what we might hear from the outside. Our "inside critics" have intimate knowledge of us and can zero in on our weakest spots.

—*Susan Ariel Rainbow Kennedy*

On Self-Criticism

Does beating up on yourself ever really help you? When I am critical with myself, it almost always leads to the same dry well of inadequacy, insecurity, and loneliness. Would we be as critical with a friend as we are with ourselves? I think not. And worse, how often do we take the misplaced irritation or grumbling out on others? If we are in recovery for doing too much, we probably are self-critical as a part of our addiction to the busyness.

We don't have to rely on others to provide us with acceptance and belonging; we can be our own source.

Today, I won't beat up on myself!

Through training there is knowledge. You can produce compassion, love, forgiveness. You can change yourself.

—*His Holiness the 14th Dalai Lama*

On Meditation

His Holiness the Dalai Lama does not want non-Buddhists to convert to Buddhism, but rather to use what can be learned through Buddhist practices. When asked specifically what he would say to burned-out doctors and health professionals in Western medicine, he recommends training of the analytical mind.

Train the mind. I always saw meditation as something mystical and out of my reach as a regular person. But what if we reframe it to training? Just like you train to run a 20K or train to participate in a sport, it is so simple that we try to make it more difficult.

Today, I will set a time to sit in silence, paying attention to my breath for three minutes. Just three minutes. I can find that amount of time. Repeat tomorrow. It is a start.

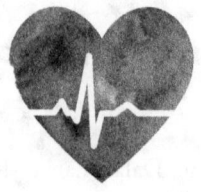

Give yourself permission to give yourself permission.

—*Unknown*

On Permission

Often, I became so busy with my practice, kids, marriage, and studies that I was exhausted. I had the feeling that if I stopped, I would never be able to start again. I dreamed of an uninterrupted bath or a night of good sleep. Yet, I made myself all kinds of wrong for even having the fantasy of escape or taking time for myself. It was like I needed permission, yet I could not provide it for myself. I never thought of giving myself permission to give myself permission.

I give you permission to give yourself permission. What? I'll say it again: You have permission to give yourself permission. It's like the first step has to be the allowing of the self to ask. We forget that we are the ones withholding our permission. No one else.

In what areas of life do you need to give yourself permission?

Today, I will repeat "I give myself permission" as a mantra. If you need to be prescribed permission, phone a friend and be sure to give her permission, too.

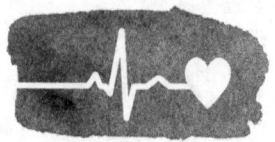

Maybe life is less about what we achieve and more about how we live moment to moment, day to day.

—*Stephanie Marston*

On Moments

Women who do too much long for quiet moments. Just moments: moments to oneself. Every Goddess (and you are the feminine energy of God/Universe, friend) requires them to source energy. To not have them makes us tired and numb and feeling like it takes tremendous energy to care for others. We are lost from our source.

Where are those quiet moments? Each of us can find moments to wake up from our numbness and resignation to take a few deep conscious breaths. To pause for even 30 seconds can bring us back to our heart-centered life force and change our whole day. New intentions and possibilities for the day may open.

I have found that 30 to 60 seconds is long enough to put my hand over my heart and breathe in God and breathe out love. This connects us with source—the source of our soul that is beyond understanding.

Today, I breathe in God and breathe out love.

Indifference and neglect often do much more damage than outright dislike.

—*J.K. Rowling*

On Relationship

How many of us are actually in relationship? Being in intimate partnership is as vulnerable as it gets. It's too easy to use busyness as an excuse to cover up our insecurities, anger at unmet expectations, or broken agreements that we know need to be addressed.

I was married and worked with my first husband. We owned our own private practice. It became easier to just talk about work and our children than to be vulnerable and really share our internal lives and love in order to keep creating intimacy. Of course, we grew apart. Get along to go along just doesn't cut it or enrich our lives. We became strangers and our relationship (and life) lost its texture and beauty.

Today, I will think of my partner/loved one and myself as two flawed human beings in an intimate dance. Aren't we lucky!

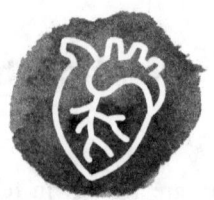

Moreover, perfectionist standards
do not allow for failure.
They do not even allow for life,
and certainly not for death.

—*Marion Woodman*

On Wholeness

Part of perfectionist's recovery is visiting the places that we think make us less than perfect. I have news for you — we are whole and perfect – just as we are.

Whole, heal, and holy are all from the same root word, hale. I am saying that we already are whole, healed, and holy. How do we do that? There is nothing to do. How do we have that? There is nothing to have. It is a way of being that you already are! There is nothing wrong or missing in your being.

Once we get a glimmer of our wholeness, we can look at our addiction to doing, doing, doing. There is no need for the crazy busyness because we already are whole, healed, and holy. We can visit new thoughts to replace the old. "I'm not good enough with "I am already whole, healed, and holy" and notice what feelings come up for us.

Today, I'll break the cycle of "I am not enough; I am not perfect; I am not...". You are whole, healed, and holy just as you are. There is nothing to do. There is nothing to have.

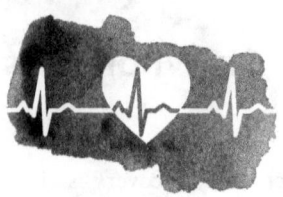

This kind of compulsive concern with "I, me, and mine" isn't the same as loving ourselves…Loving ourselves points us to the capacities of resilience, compassion, and understanding within that are simply part of being alive.

—*Sharon Salzberg*

On Self-Compassion

Self-compassion starts with the awareness that we are suffering—that things are really hard right now. We have to feel our suffering rather than resist it or block it out of our minds. We must be willing to observe our negative emotions and thoughts with clarity. Once we recognize the suffering, we can bring compassion and kindness to ourselves and remember that our suffering is an experience in common with all other human beings. We deserve kindness.

I must remind myself. I am guilty of speaking to myself with unkind words.

How do you speak to yourself? Do you treat yourself with kindness?

Today is a good day to start.

I've seen that mixture of resignation and hopelessness before; it's usually in my mirror.

—*Mira Grant*

On Resignation

I believe there is an epidemic of resignation. Surely, we take on tasks we don't like and then are resigned to the fact that we are stuck with them. That is typical for women who do too much.

Yet, we want to resist resignation, ignore it, and pretend it is not there. Maybe our resignation is about our career, a relationship, or other area of our lives. It is there and will continue to be until we embrace and bring loving kindness to the resignation in ourselves. (We can also embrace the resignation of others, bringing loving kindness.) When we bring love to our resignation, freedom to create solutions is possible because we are no longer pushing against it while pretending all is well.

You can't create on top of avoiding, defending, resisting, or pretending because whatever we resist, persists. When we find ourselves working too much, we might ask the question: Am I running away from my resignation? What am I resigned about? How can I love that part of me? What can I change?

Today, I will slow down and take an honest inventory of places in my life where I am resigned, and I'll bring love to them. Only then is change possible.

PRAYER

Father, Mother, God,

May I have peace

May I have happiness

May I have equanimity

May I have love.

May all sentient beings have love.

Amen

I imagine that the intelligent people are the ones so intelligent that they don't even need or want to look "intelligent" anymore.

—*Criss Jami*

On Humility

I think women in medicine, more than men, have to be aware of the appearance of intelligence—constantly looking the part. It is a survival mechanism, but it can become a habit and is exhausting! What would happen if you gave up looking "intelligent" to just be yourself? May I remind you how intelligent you have to be to get where you are today?

It is humility to know your own intelligence, your own worth. This is authentic, the knowing, the being. Then one does not have to act at all. There is so much time left over and room to think of others, instead of myself.

Today, I will remind myself that I am intelligent, capable, competent, and worthy. If I don't have to think of myself, I can be in the world with ease and grace.

[My dog is] faithful, loving, valuable, warm, nurturing, intelligent, affectionate, and capable of ripping someone who attacks me or my loved ones to ribbons. She's a bitch, and, except for the way she drools and sheds, I want to be just like her.

—*Ellen Snortland*

On Patriarchy

It is important to note that we are living in a male-dominated world. However, we must not believe the patriarchy is the absolute truth. Patriarchy is not THE truth that we are stuck with. We can start living authentically, consciously, and from our own personal power to bring our work, our compassion, and our love to bear on the world. Think of how different the world might look if we made this shift. A whole new world is possible. That is who we truly are.

Today, authenticity is my truth.

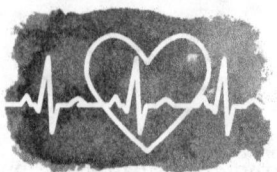

Anger will never disappear so long as thoughts of resentment are cherished in the mind.

—*Buddha*

On Resentment

What are resentments? They are unmet expectations that are swallowed like poison. Accumulated resentments are the end of a relationship. There is nothing more toxic to our self and our relationships.

It is an expression of love to communicate unmet needs that we expected another person to provide. Otherwise, we are placing blame on another person, and they didn't even know they did something wrong! Resentment is also placing our power over there with another person and then blaming them for our loss of power.

I can't have a great marriage, partnership, or friendship if I am not willing to express what I need, keep a check on expectations, and communicate disappointments or unmet needs. Otherwise, we poison the relationship and ourselves, and we give our power away.

Resentments and blame make us sick.

Today, I will let go.

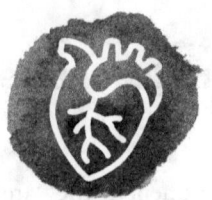

The space that isn't an absence but a presence. A pause that is bigger than the noise that surrounds it. A gap that is a mirror. A gulf that is a bridge. The emptiness that is rejuvenating. The space that is full of more than it could ever contain.

—*Helen Rickerby*

On Quiet Moments

I enjoy and need my quiet moments now. I can remember being a too-busy physician, raising four children, and being a good-enough wife who craved just a few quiet moments. If I could soak in a tub with my wine, uninterrupted, it would have been my idea of heaven. Of course, any mother knows luxurious baths don't happen very often, if at all, and I think eventually I kind of lost myself because I was so busy doing and not being. The cost? Me.

The road back to myself required quiet moments. Moments to breathe in the Divine and breathe out the bullshit distractions. Quiet moments to sit with the soul. Private moments with nature or a good friend. These are requirements for our recovery. They are like the ABCs of resuscitation.

A: Awareness: Clear the shit of the external world.

B: Breathe deeply.

C: Calm: Feel your heart rate slow.

I have found that even 30 to 60 seconds of breathing makes a huge difference.

Today, I'll prioritize a few quiet moments. My recovery depends on it.

Meditations for Women Physicians (and Others) Who Do Too Much

PRAYER

Father, Mother, God,

Grant me compassion for myself.

Help me to free my soul from the bounds I've placed,

To cherish my uniqueness,

To be in awe of myself

As part of a sacred whole.

Let me be motivated by Love,

And my own self-acceptance.

Amen

As women, we
have super powers.
We are sisters.
We are healers.
We are mothers.
We are goddess warriors.

—*Merle Dandridge*

On Strength

So, I have an inner bitch. She is like my superpower. She is my confidence. Not every person will have a bitch as their superpower, but we all possess that inner quality of confidence, strength, and personal power. She may be a part of yourself that you are familiar with, or she may be a stranger. Either way, I know that she is there when called upon. The trick is remembering.

Today, I'll look for my inner bitch/superpower and ask her to tea.

You are only as limited as your beliefs.

—*Jennifer Ho-Dougatz*

On Limiting Beliefs

Where do beliefs come from? Belief in one's authentic, wonderful, and free self means examining old beliefs that do not serve you.

Limiting beliefs travel with a lot of shoulds, buts, musts, can'ts, nots, and don'ts. Beware when you hear them in your thinking and speaking. Ask yourself: What is the belief I have? Where did that belief come from? Whose belief is it anyway? Is this belief mine or from some other source (culture, parents, family, friends, teachers, religion, to name a few places these beliefs might belong)? Does this belief set me free or keep me caged in my indoctrination?

You get to decide if the belief really serves you or if it is even your own belief. If it doesn't serve you, let it go. If it is not yours, let it go or send it back to the owner with love. It's not yours to have to keep. You get to decide.

Today, I'll pay attention to the shoulds, buts, musts, can'ts, nots, and don'ts as a clue to a limiting belief that I may or may not want to keep. I will send those that don't serve me or belong to me away with love.

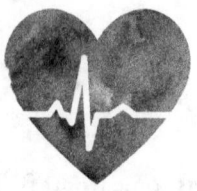

There they were, keeping the world in order ... by sitting on the mystery of life and knowing themselves that there was no mystery.

—*Isak Dinesen*

On Life

My mother and one of my best friends died within a month of each other, my father had heart surgery, my own business was spookily quiet, and then a pandemic started. To resist against life is futile and exhausting. No matter how hard we try, we cannot control everyone and everything in life.

This is part of being a recovering perfectionist. We get frustrated when it doesn't go our way, or we get it just right and something comes along to change it.

Life is life-ing. The only other alternative is dying. We can learn to be responsible for what is in our power, but we cannot stop the divine mystery of life ever changing

That is life.

Today, I'll give up the hamster wheel of my fantasy perfect life and accept that life is life-ing. Really, it's perfect, just the way it is

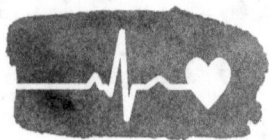

Moral injury describes the challenge of simultaneously knowing what care patients need but being unable to provide it due to constraints that are beyond our control.

—*Wendy Dean, MD*

On Moral Injury

It is exhausting participating in systems that we know do not work or do not work well. We are asked to do things that we know are not for the highest good of our patients, ourselves, or our families. What is the choice we have? It can make us feel powerless, and we may react by numbing on the sofa, or by doing, doing, doing. Either way, we do not want to face the feelings of our moral injury.

We cannot simply ignore this exhaustion; exhaustion is the cloak of sadness. We grieve that the systems cannot do better. It is not your fault. It is not my fault, yet it feels like we are complicit. This is not our truth.

It is ok to feel this sadness of injury. It is ok to stay in the system. It is ok to leave. There is no right answer—only what will work for us.

Today, I will have compassion for my injury and grief.

For those who see it, the butterfly brings beauty to the world. It also shows us humans that transformation is a common and natural part of life's process.

—*Louise Hart*

On Transformation

The butterfly brings not only beauty, but also grace. When the worm is in cocoon, it has no idea what is in store for it, how it will look, or that it will take a trip flying thousands of miles. It is in the blind.

As with the butterfly, much of our growth and development comes from our blind spots.

There is FAR more that we don't know than what we do know. When we know something, we know that we know it. Or we can know that we don't know something and learn about it, so we do know. The tricky part is not knowing what we don't know. There is a whole new world and possibilities available when we, through coaching, distinguish what we don't know that we don't know—our blind spots. A whole new world awaits.

Today, I am opening myself to have my blind spots revealed to me so I can transform.

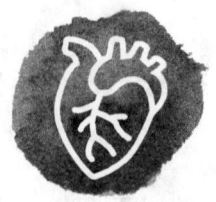

Wanna fly, you got to give up the shit that weighs you down.

—*Toni Morrison*

On Letting Go

Is there something you need to let go of? Perhaps you need radical self-forgiveness for something you are holding onto. What is that thing? Can you write it down, or put it into words? I am upset because_____. I need to forgive myself for _____. What are your judgements about yourself regarding this "something"? What beliefs need challenging? What have you made the situation mean about you? Is it really true? What stops you from releasing these thoughts of self-condemnation? What are your reasons, rationalizations, and excuses for not forgiving yourself?

Do you really need to hold onto those thoughts from the past? As long as we hold on, the past is shaping our future. Letting go can create space, a sense of freedom and lightness, and peace.

Today, I am making a list of things I that I need to forgive myself for. I am taking one situation/event and writing everything there is to write about it, and then let it go. Let it go. Let it go...

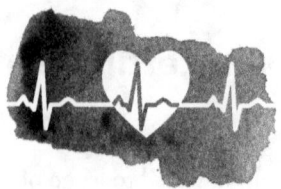

Growth is a spiral process, doubling back on itself, reassessing, and regrouping.

—*Julia Margaret Cameron*

On Recovery

I am a recovering perfectionist, smoker, fixaholic, careaholic, woman who does too much. Recovery is a process like an infinite sacred spiral, like a labyrinth. You walk a circular path to the center, then walk outward in ever-enlarging circles. This is our sacred rhythm. We contract inward, and we flow outward, ever expanding.

The next time you have the opportunity to walk a labyrinth, meditate as you walk, going inward to grow outward. For now, draw spirals on everything. Start outside and draw the spiral inward and then draw from the inside out.

As a person in recovery, I am always contracting inward and expanding outward for continual growth in sacred rhythm.

Today, I'll take time to go inward to face outward.

And while we wait in silence for that final luxury of fearlessness, the weight of that silence will choke us.

—*Audre Lorde*

On Fear and Anxiety

What makes us afraid to speak up or take on the things we want to do and the causes we want to champion? All of us have fear. Audre Lorde had fear—genuine fear of bodily harm as a Black, lesbian female in the 1960s and 70s.

But some of us operate from fear most of the time, even when there is no real danger. We may keep too busy or drink that extra glass of wine to blunt the sensation of daily fear. I have had that second or third glass of wine to self-medicate my own daily fears: fear of failure, fear of someone not liking me, fear of not being perfect.

If there is no bodily danger, fear is a constellation of thoughts (many times about a future that hasn't even happened yet) that generate a feeling and a body response. If we can sit with this body reaction (and yes, it is uncomfortable) and notice the associated thoughts and their patterns, we can reframe them.

I am not saying this is easy, but fear keeps us silent too much of the time. It stifles our soul and chokes our self-expression.

Today, I'll take inventory of fear-based thoughts that suppress my self-expression in the world.

It's one of the greatest gifts
you can give yourself, to forgive.
Forgive everybody.

—*Maya Angelou*

On Forgiveness

For an exercise, start with a relationship you think could be better, you want to be better, or should be better. Consider a relationship where you feel disappointed, angry, or betrayed. You need to be committed to forgiveness, so if it's something you want to hold onto and not ready to let it go, its ok. Choose an easier one.

How has that relationship been since the event? Is it in the space between you? Is it that you want to continue to punish this person, cut off love or respect, or feel badly about it? Have you written them off? Do you know you need to give it up because it weighs you down? Is it poisoning your soul?

What would it look like to have everything as before the event? Would life be lighter? Carrying around the weight of a past of unforgiveness (and this includes unforgiveness for yourself) is exhausting.

I have found that I have a choice to forgive or not forgive. It is in our power to alter the future of who we are being in relationship to ourselves and others.

Today, I am willing to forgive.

PRAYER

Father, Mother, God

Let my thoughts be freed

And shine radiantly from my mind

May each dark thought be illuminated

To be kissed by the sun,

Loved by the moon

To float away transformed

Amen

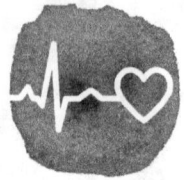

For now, she need not think of anybody. She could be herself, by herself. And that was what now she often felt the need of: to think; well not even to think. To be silent; to be alone.

—*Virginia Woolf*

On Solitude

My mother used to make me rest in the afternoons when I was a child. I am sure she needed the time to rest from parenting in those afternoon "naps," but she would send me off to my room saying, "You need to learn to be by yourself, Robyn." What wisdom. I see now.

In the quietness of my mind, I can process. I can feel my feelings. I can get to know myself. I can be creative. I can travel to far lands. I can ground spiritually. Being addicted to busyness and work takes away a whole world, another whole life of my inner self.

Today, I'll savor moments alone and make that solitude a priority to full living.

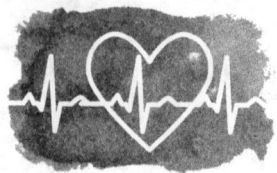

All of us are afraid sometimes, that's human. When our life is ruled by fear, that's addiction.

—*Anne Wilson Schaef*

On Fear

Do you come home exhausted? Perhaps you're addicted to fear. It does have us amped up with temporary energy—like a hit of a drug. Fear, as Anne Wilson Schaef says, is a natural part of being human. However, unchecked fear is addiction.

In seeking to be perfect, I can become obsessively fearful about whatever the situation is and, all of a sudden, fear is driving the whole show while I mentally and emotionally check out. Sometimes I am not aware that I have been in a fear state until I come home exhausted.

For me, the fear/anxiety spiral starts with stress, then underlying fear causes more stress, which causes more fear, and it continues. Wah la! I am in the fear cyclone, and my life is unmanageable. At these times, I stop, take a breath, and trust the process and my higher power.

Today, I will simply be aware of my breath when I experience stress or find myself in the downward spiral of fear. The first step is awareness.

"Bitch. Noun. Though formal definitions dictate a worthless woman, a shameful she-devil, a heinous hellcat, a shrill shrew, a curse of a cunt, or someone of the like. We all know a man wrote that shit.

—*Britt Greifeld*

On Inner Bitch Work

I've been called a bitch and posit that that word has been whispered about me more than I know. As women physicians, we have to be nice and pleasing all while working harder than our male colleagues to advance and be respected. We have to give ourselves a bit of a break!

What if "bitch" was a power word? A word not for apology. What if each woman had a "bitch manifesto" that is a collection of power words. Yes, it is the inner power to stop taking shit—for expressing displeasure at being overlooked, for speaking our minds with a certain tone so people will listen. If that is what "bitch" means, count me in.

Today, I refuse to be put down, overlooked, ignored, or dismissed. Bring it on, bitch!

Should is a futile word. It's about what didn't happen. It belongs in a parallel universe. It belongs in another dimension of space.

—*Margaret Atwood*

On Shoulds

Do you "should" on yourself? "Should" is a nasty word when we do. I should do this. I should be that. I should of... The word can turn into a big club to beat ourselves with. Or it can become a club others can beat us with.

What would happen if we replace should with could? I could do this. I could be this. I could of... That gives a person more room to breathe and consider options, not should haves.

When I paid attention to my vocabulary, I found "should" all over the place. I am careful now how I use this word. I am probably more adept at not using it with others than myself. It's a sneaky, sneaky word.

Today, I'll stop shoulding on myself and others.

Shame is a nonfunctional emotion.

—*Wise friend of the author*

On Shame

I carried shame around the death of one of my patients. Had I done everything? Did I do it right? What would my peers say? Would they sue? Am I a good doctor? An elder General Practitioner friend of mine used to tell me that I was using shame to beat myself up and evade being responsible for my life. My thoughts and feelings of shame had me see myself as not worthy. Why would God, Jesus, Buddha, the Universe (whoever you pray to) want that for you? We ARE worthy! It is okay to feel bad about something we did or didn't do, but it is not okay to carry it around, internalize it, or direct it to our being.

Guilt says, "I did something wrong." Shame says, "I am wrong."

If we step back and observe the shame that we hold on to and how and who we are being when burdened by that shame, we realize that it weighs us down, makes us want to numb out, and makes us cranky. We might want to be "too busy" to avoid the feelings of shame.

Shame is constricting and not congruent with growth. And life is about growing.

Today, I ask myself, what shame am I holding onto that is serving no purpose? Can I now forgive myself and let it go?

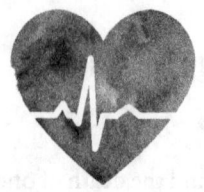

You may believe that you are responsible for what you do, but not for what you think. The truth is that you are responsible for what you think because it is only at this level that you can exercise choice. What you do comes from what you think.

—*Marianne Williamson*

On Thoughts

When faced with difficult times, we might react to circumstances in a negative way. It is not the circumstance that determines how we react. It is our thoughts and the things we tell ourselves (our story) about the circumstances that determine our reactions, behavior, and physiology. Choosing our thoughts starts with paying attention to self-talk. We all have that running commentary in our heads. We get to choose what we listen to: the blah, blah, blah of self-criticism and negativity or the conscious sage who has our best interests in mind and reacts with kindness, optimism, and generosity.

So, where is your thinking getting you into trouble? Where are you reacting instead of consciously choosing your thoughts and actions? Are you aware of the running commentary inside your head? Is that inner voice mostly negative or is it optimistic? You get to decide!

Today, I'll watch my thoughts and ignore the blah, blah, blah and negativity. I can change my thoughts.

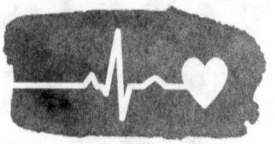

Deciding what not to do is as important as deciding what to do.

—*Jessica Jackley*

On Trust

Many of us are good at doing things ourselves and less inclined to accept the help of others. We, as busyaholics (and I include myself in here), may complain that we feel like we are doing more than others, always taking care of others' needs before our own and feel put-upon, possibly resentful. We have created our own lives of being in charge, doing it better, and working harder and longer than perhaps our male colleagues or other members of the healthcare team. It is a badge of honor to be the hardest working, the one to work the longest hours and be the most productive.

But our worth is not defined by our productivity! Let me repeat that: Our worth is not defined by our productivity! We must learn to stop looking outside of ourselves for our worth and instead find it within.

When we find our own worth, trusting another to do something we need done—i.e. delegating or asking for help—becomes easier.

Today, I'll use "My worth is not defined by my productivity" as a mantra and reminder to listen within and trust.

Loving ourselves works miracles in our lives.

—*Louise Hay*

On Self-Love

We do too much, and we always have a reason: "This is a priority!" "And this is a priority." "Don't miss this; it's important!" "You need to worry about this, and this and this." Plus, you worry about all of it. You get my point. The distractions of the world can suck you in. The hard part is that we don't even notice. Where is the center? It's like being pulled into various scenarios when we should be pulling inward first—to our own hearts. A scattered self is not effective or loving. A love for ourselves makes us heart centered.

Today, I will put my hand on my heart and bring awareness to my heart center before loving others.

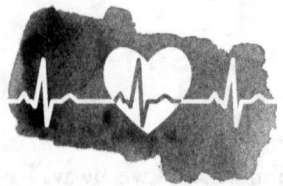

We find greater lightness and ease in our lives as we increasingly care for ourselves and other beings.

—*Sharon Salzberg*

On Self-Compassion

I learned in Buddhism that one must show compassion for oneself before you can show compassion to others. You must care for yourself before you care for others. Likewise, If I am good to others, but disparage myself, then the good to others rings hollow. It is not real; it is incongruent, and I feel the hollowness of being separate from others.

Separation causes loneliness—a place far from the feeling of belonging, oneness, or interconnection. When we feel this loneliness of separation, we tend to take on working more, looking busier, searching for perfection. We may take on caring for others to the detriment of ourselves—and then resent all the needy people in our lives.

I am perfect just the way I am. Self-compassion and care of the self allows me to be compassionate and care for others.

I will follow that system of regimen, which, according to my ability and judgment, I consider for the benefit of my patients, and abstain from whatever is deleterious and mischievous.

—*Hippocrates*

On Humility

There is a line of care where we actually disempower and harm our patients because we have the arrogance to make them wrong, rather than inform, educate, and offer to partner with them. We do not know what is going on in their lives and hearts. Yet, we act like we do. An assumption is made that we know better than them. Really, they are the experts of their own bodies!

A shift in our thinking allows us to work as a team with patients. That added connection heals and is good for our own souls. This is much better than the alternative world of make-wrong, which serves to isolate and alienate.

Arrogance kills. Humility heals.

Today, I will let folks be the expert in their own lives. Humility heals.

My "awakened dreams" are about shifts. Thought shifts, reality shifts, gender shifts: one person metamorphoses into another in a world where people fly through the air, heal from mortal wounds. I am playing with my Self, I am playing with the world's soul, I am the dialogue between my Self, and el espiritu del mundo. I change myself, I change the world.

—*Gloria E Anzaldua*

On Transformation

In the world of the study of being human, transformation is likened to metamorphosis, or thorough and complete change in beliefs so that actions become natural and achieve the desired result in life. I liken it to discovering your beliefs, thoughts, and feelings in areas of the self that are there but unknown—the discovery of the authentic self and the soul's purpose and power. Once discovered, new and desired futures can be envisioned and brought to fruition.

Today, I am willing to see things differently—newly.

Cherish your solitude. Take trains by yourself to places you have never been. Sleep out alone under the stars. Learn how to drive a stick shift. Go so far away that you stop being afraid of not coming back. Say no when you don't want to do something. Say yes if your instincts are strong, even if everyone around you disagrees. Decide whether you want to be liked or admired. Decide if fitting in is more important than finding out what you're doing here. Believe in kissing.

—*Eve Ensler*

On Solitude

I love this quote: "Cherish your solitude" is something I dreamed of, but never made happen until I was burned out. When we're in busyness, we don't know what we're missing. We don't see that solitude is a requirement of the soul. It is what allows life to be rich and textured. To give up solitude is to give up a whole inner world.

It may be uncomfortable at first, but a whole world, be it stillness or adventure, is available in those places of solitude.

Today, I'll find solitude to cherish.

"We must say "no" to what, in our heart, we don't want. We must say "no" to doing things out of obligation, thereby cheating those important to us of the purest expression of our love. We must say "no" to treating ourselves, our health, our needs as not as important as someone else's. We must say "no."

—*Suzette R. Hinton*

On Saying "No"

Try this. Say "no" out loud. It feels low, deep and stern (in my mind anyway). Say "yes" and see how it is shallower, light, and almost melodic. I posit that it is naturally more difficult to say "no." Trouble saying "no" is ubiquitously common in women physicians who do too much. And it is a critical skill for our recovery.

We have flaccid "no" muscles after years of saying "yes." Practice saying "no" with a friend. Remember how easy it is for a small child to say an emphatic "no"! You can do it!

Today, I'll practice the art of saying "no."

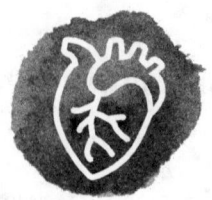

Life's under no obligation to give us what we expect.

—*Margaret Mitchell*

On Expectations

I expected the perfect marriage, career, and life in general. Boy, was I disappointed!

Let us count the ways that expectations are killers. We kill ourselves trying to meet the unrealistic expectations that we have for ourselves. We kill relationships with those we love with unvoiced, unmet expectations. Life becomes joyless and dead when we expect outcomes fashioned in our minds that life does not deliver.

Expectations of women in this current time set us up for failure. We can never be that perfect woman, mother, wife, daughter, doctor.

So why do we still expect so much?

Women who do too much forget that people (particularly those we love) cannot read our minds. Just because we have high expectations of ourselves does not mean others have the same expectations. We live in expectation mismatch. How lonely that is.

Today, I'll try living connected with others and look for the gifts life already gives.

[...] it was like a big, incredible tapestry that just happened to— if you could decipher it—tell a million little stories from my life.

—*Eve O. Schaub*

On Uniqueness

Life is like a tapestry composed of individual threads that are different colors, dark, light, smooth, rough, neat, and frayed. If you think of each of these threads as a moment in time of your life, then just like the tapestry, variation is required for it to be a beautiful piece of art. If all the threads were uniform, we would have just a rug and that is boring. Likewise, if all our moments are the same, without highs and lows, lightness and darkness, happiness, and sadness, then life would be boring. We need these variations to live a full and beautiful human life. Then we can learn to appreciate and be present for them all. We can eventually learn to hold it all.

Today, I am present to my life without having to change a thing. All is appreciated.

Life is a success of moments. To live each one is to succeed.

—*Corita Kent*

On Success

We know logically that we can define success externally with career and materialism. I have been successful. I wouldn't be a doctor if I wasn't, and so have you. I've gotten accolades from others: awards and kind words. Is that success? How else can we define success?

What if we look at it as *being* successful? If I were being success, there would be room for qualities such as joy, grace, and gratitude. Each moment would depend on living a conscious and self-aware life.

Who would you be if you were to *be* success? Would you appreciate every moment? Be less stressed? Would you be able to sit quietly with yourself, knowing that you matter intrinsically? It is not your career, your prestige and power, your things, your marriage, your children. Being a unique expression of the divine is enough. You are enough.

Today, how do I define success in my life? I am successful.

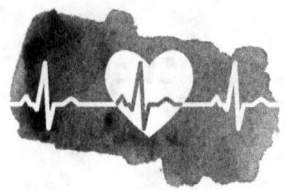

Your thoughts are like the seeds you plant in your garden. Your beliefs are like the soil in which you plant these seeds.

—*Louise Hay*

On Limiting Beliefs

I once believed that I couldn't be the one to start a women's clinic on a medical mission to the remote Himalayas. At some point, after many prayers, I had to give up that thought and associated fear, or it would never happen. Unexamined beliefs can keep you from your best life and your best self.

Limiting beliefs are formed in childhood and associated with difficult emotions. They arise automatically when you are in challenging circumstances. The belief came from your parents, or your family, or society, or your friends.

A limiting belief is associated with an emotion, so if you find yourself with an unwanted emotion, such as fear as I did, you can challenge the associated thoughts and underlying beliefs. Once you identify a limiting belief, you can bring it into the light and decide if it really yours, if it is really true. You can imagine the mealy garden that would result from soil of limiting beliefs.

Today, it is time for you to bloom and blossom as outrageous colors of you!

Practice the pause. Pause before judging. Pause before assuming. Pause before accusing. Pause whenever you're about to react harshly, and you'll avoid doing and saying things you'll later regret.

—*Lori Deschene*

On Pause

My mother used to advise that I count to 10 in my head before reacting to naughty behavior of one of my children. I would remember this many times. (Children are such great teachers!) She was teaching me the power of the pause.

When I am triggered, I get a particular feeling in my body right before I am about to react. I feel a flash of anger and then like my breath is caught at my throat and the area around my solar plexus feels tight. It is my signal that I am about to go down a path that I might regret. The pause is the exhale and relaxation my body. I find it useful to know these key feelings and body responses because it gives me more agency and choice in my life.

In Buddhism and mindfulness practice, the pause is a tool to bring us back to the present moment, to center ourselves, to be at choice. In this way, our consciousness can catch up to the automatic thought and behavior patterns. It is allowing—allowing the moment. We simply take a breath and exhale into the now.

Remember, it is a practice. You'll fail many times!

Today, I'll count to 10 and breathe during tense moments.

Meditation List

For Calm/Peace

On Acceptance	15
On Adrenaline	29
On Arrogance	73
On Beginning Meditation	53
On Being versus Doing	67
On Busyness	85
On Clarity	97
On Control	109
On Delegating	121
On Expectations	207
On Meditation	135
On Moments	139
On Pause	215
On Permission	137
On Quiet Moments	157
On Recovery	173
On Solitude	181, 203

For Comfort/Cheering Up

On Crying	17
On Getting Unstuck	31
On Perception	55
On Resignation	147
On Tears	111

For Connection

On Our Ancestors	19
On Comfort	33
On Compassion	43
On Emotions	57
On Estrangement	69
On Expectations	87
On Fixing People	99
On Listening	113, 123
On Relationship	141
On Resentment	155
On Trust	193

For Faith

On a Power Greater Than Ourselves	21
On Awe	45, 71
On Belief	115
On Goddess	125

For Forgiveness

On Anger	23
On Forgiveness	35, 59, 75, 89, 177
On Guilt	127
On Letting Go	171
On Shame	189

For Joy/Happiness/Purpose

On Conformity	25
On Happiness	37
On Humor	47
On Integrity	61
On Intuition	79
On Muchness	91
On Purpose	101
On Projects	129
On Uniqueness	209

For Self-Compassion

On Being Human	105
On Comparison	39
On Exhaustion	49, 81
On Failure	63
On First Steps	13
On Mini Meditations	93
On Perfection	11
On Perfectionism and Procrastination	117
On Saying "No"	103, 205
On Self-Compassion	145, 197
On Self-Love	131, 195
On Self-Criticism	133
On Shoulds	187
On Thoughts	191
On Wholeness	143

For Strength/Confidence

On Awareness	27
On Badassness	41
On Being Uncomfortable	51
On Being Unmesswithable	83
On Courage	95
On Everyday Courage	107
On Fear	119, 183
On Fear/Anxiety	173
On Humility	151, 199
On Inner Bitch Work	185
On Limiting Beliefs	163, 213
On Patriarchy	153
On Self-Worth	65
On Strength	161
On Success	211
On Transformation	169, 201

MISC

On Life	165
On Moral Injury	167

For More Support

I am a doctor, but not your doctor. None of the contents of this book is to be construed as me giving medical advice. I am a physician coach and believe in the power of coaching, but not at the exclusion of proper medical care and therapy.

There is a physician specific helpline that is staffed by volunteer psychiatrists that is free and confidential to support physicians with mental health issues. **Physician Support Line** (888) 409-0141.

If you need or desire life coaching support and don't know where to start, I highly recommend a group that I helped to cofound, Physician Coaching Alliance (PCA) at https://physiciancoachingalliance.com. There you can find coaches for individuals, groups, and institutions. Physician Coach Support at https://physiciancoachsupport.com is also a good resource, and I currently volunteer there.

Other organizations that I recommend include American Medical Women's Association coaching program, Coaching for Institutions, Physician Coaching Institute, and Empowering Women Physicians. For mama docs, check out Physicians Moms Group on Facebook.

Of course, I would love to be your coach! You can find my coaching practice at https://www.dralley-hay.com/. I am happy to connect and explore if coaching is for you. You can also find me on Facebook: https://www.facebook.com/dralleyhay, Instagram: https://www.instagram.com/dralleyhay.coach, and LinkedIn: https://www.linkedin.com/in/life-coach-robyn-alley-hay.
Email: dralleyhay@gmail.com

Acknowledgments

To my husband, Mark Wooldridge, your steadfastness, love, and care have given me the space and encouragement I needed to write and to pursue my chosen second career. Thank you for believing in me, Love. I am so grateful I found you.

Thank you to my four children. Motherhood can only be described as the highest of the highs and the lowest of the lows in life, and a mother's love is deep and forever. Each of you continues to bless my life.

Thank you to my mother, posthumously, for the life lessons you've taught. For my dad, who taught me I could be whoever I wanted to be.

Thank you to my sister-in-law, Sara, for being my "Sis" and friend. We've shared about our life's lessons over glasses of wine many times. I treasure those moments. Darin, I love you, too.

Thank you to my writing group Genice, Crystal, Lisa, Niroo, Mayri, and our fearless leader and writing coach Ellen Snortland for listening to my meditations as they were being created. Your input was always positive and gave me the courage to share it with a larger audience. Ellen, you are inspiring in many ways, as an author, columnist, playwrite, rebel, and most importantly, an activist for women everywhere.

Thank you to the rock star Physician Coaches at Physician Coaching Alliance: Doctors Errin Weisman, Kara Pepper, Susan Wilson, Tracy Assamoah, Tracey O'Connell, and Melissa Hankins to name a few. You all have no idea how much the community and your friendship mean to me!

Thank you to Valerie Hellerman and Hands On Global, inc. for allowing me to continue to put my medical knowledge to good use. You are inspiring in your work for humanity. I am forever changed.

Thank you to all the lovely people of Zanskar, India. Your demonstration of happiness, compassion, and wisdom inspires me. I receive so much more than I give.

Finally, I thank Jennifer Bright and Bright Communications for your patience with editing and getting a book out of all of my disorganized files and Anna Magruder for taking my ideas and making them real. The artwork is kick-ass.

About the Author

Robyn Alley-Hay, MD, is an international women's empowerment coach, physician coach, speaker, and author. Her interests include working with doctors (and others) who are up to something, whether that be entering leadership, taking on a large project, or having a balanced and fulfilled life as a doctor and a mother. Power, purpose, and clarity are the bedrock of her coaching process and leadership and communication skills are the vehicle.

She is a graduate of the University of Kansas School of Medicine, did her residency in Obstetrics and Gynecology at the University of Kansas, Wichita, is a Certified Physician Development Coach with Physician Coaching Institute, cofounder of Physician Coaching Alliance, and a Fellow at the Harvard affiliated Institute of Coaching. She also works with a nonprofit that, at the invitation of the Dalai Lama, provides western medicine to a Tibetan Buddhist population in the far reaches of the Himalayan mountains.

As a mother of four grown children, Dr. Alley-Hay knows well the challenges of being a physician mom. She is currently living and loving in the Dallas, Texas, area with her husband, two longhorn cows, nine goats, two dogs, several cats, and chickens, and one duck.

Dr. Alley-Hay can be reached on social media or at her website DrAlley-Hay.com for speaking, coaching, and consulting inquiries.

www.ingramcontent.com/pod-product-compliance
Lightning Source LLC
Chambersburg PA
CBHW050315120526
44592CB00014B/1923